SEASONS OF CHANGE

GENE R. JOHNSTON

Gotham Books

30 N Gould St.
Ste. 20820, Sheridan, WY 82801
https://gothambooksinc.com/

Phone: 1 (307) 464-7800

© 2024 *Gene R. Johnston*. All rights reserved.

No part of this book may be reproduced, stored in a retrieval system, or transmitted by any means without the written permission of the author.

Published by Gotham Books (October 2, 2024)

ISBN: 979-8-88775-656-1 (H)
ISBN: 979-8-88775-654-7 (P)
ISBN: 979-8-88775-655-4 (E)

Because of the dynamic nature of the Internet, any web addresses or links contained in this book may have changed since publication and may no longer be valid.

The views expressed in this work are solely those of the author and do not necessarily reflect the views of the publisher, and the publisher hereby disclaims any responsibility for them.

If you are reading this book, I have a few words of wisdom for you.

First off, in these pages, I have tried to convey my thoughts of hope, joy, love, and loss.
I also have tried to share my thoughts on how important contentment is to each of us.

Someone once told me that life is not about the past nor is it about the future. Life is about the here and now and making as much of it as you can. I am here to tell you that they are 100% right.

I have seen too many people in my life living in the past or are so wrapped up in trying to live such a dream of the future that they have in their heads. And not one of these people is truly happy with what they have right in front of them.

A change of seasons is coming to humanity. Our society is now filled with so much hatred and bitterness for ourselves and each other that it's hard to find any contentment.

Yes, the seasons of change are upon us and we must choose how we are to live, will it be (in hatred and bitterness or love and compassion)?

Gene R. Johnston

Dedication

I dedicate this book to all those who have inspired me to write.

Katherine Johnston (my Mom), Patrica Turner (my sister), Melvin Johnston (my Dad), Annie Berry, Abigail Keen, and many more. Over the years these people have encouraged me to read more and to put down what is in my head.

TABLE OF CONTENTS

Dedication	vi
Seasons of Change	1
Miracles do happen that's All I Know	3
Out of the Darkness & Into the Light	4
To my Dad	5
Oh my Love	6
The Myth	7
The Pathfinder	8
God of Wonders	10
Oh Lord my God	11
Your Prayers	12
I Can only Imagine	13
God's Love for You	14
The Gift	15
Mother's Prayers	16
Be Thou my Vision	17
The River of Love	18
Better Now	19
Somewhere over the Horizon	20
Deep Love	21
Undying Love	22
A Future Together	23
Step by Step	24
This Thing called Love	25
Not with Me	26
Searching the Horizon	27
A New Life	28
To Father	29
Daybreak	30
Changed My Life	31
To my True Love	32
The Depth of Love	33
Dreamed a Dream	34
A New Song	35
Message of Love	36
To my Wife	37
Lonely Heart	38
My Greatest Wish	39
Searching for you	40
Good Morning my Love	41
Loving you openly	42
My Dearest:	43
Limitless Love	44
My little Moon Shadow	45
Mom & Dad	46
Every Night	47

The River of Love	48
I Will Walk with You	49
Yesterday	50
By Loving Me	51
From the First Look	52
Bound in Love	53
A Morning like No Other	54
My Dearest Loving Husband	55
My Love for You	56
Words from Your Lips	57
Longing for You	58
Daily Journeys	59
Let Go of the Past	60
How to Measure a Person Worth	61
Idea of Freedom	62
Loving You	63
Distant Light	64
Your Touch	65
Christ in Me	66
Hand in Hand	67
The Prayer	68
Feel My Love	69
Trust in You	70
Magic of Love	71
Good morning Sweetheart!	72
Hear These Words	73
Your Presence	74
The Darkness	75
Morning Comes	76
When I see you	77
One Love	78
You are the Key	79
The Sword of the Lord	80
To My Precious Angel	81
Bright Eyes	82
Your Eyes	83
Stories of your Love	84
Boundless Love	85
Counting my Blessings	86
I Take Comfort	87
God of Wonders	88
My Little Angel	89
Look into my Eyes	90
Power of Love	91
Sending You My Love	92
The Love I have	93
Thinking of You	94

Wayward Child	95
Yesterday, Today, & Tomorrow	96
Your Magic	97
You're the One	98
Upward and Onward	99
I Hear Your Tender Whispers	100
Life Fulfilled	101
Only You	103
Life with you	104
Without You	105
Miracles Do Happen	106
To my Beloved Sister	107
I Chose to Love You	108
Take me	109
Take my Hand	110
Every night	111
Angels Sing	112
Your Love Lifts Me Up	113
I will love you	114
Little House	115
Letting Go of the Father's hand	116
Evidence of my Love	117
Fingerprints	118
Distant stars	119
Quite of the Night	120
Divine Illumination	121
Embracing Eternity	122
Steadfast Companion (1)	123
Steadfast Companion (2)	124
Eternal Yearning	125
Ethereal Odyssey	126
Divine Nature's Embrace	127
Sacred Tapestry	128
Echoes of the Soul	129
Whispers of Love	130
A Journey from Loneliness to Hope	131
Eternal Devotion	132
Song for over the horizon	133
God's Gift	138
Author's Message	140
The Plan of Salvation	141
Who paid the price?	142
What is the way out?	142
How can I get out?	143

Seasons of Change

The season of change has come into my life once again, and it has made my life fertile ground for your love to grow within.

Just as life begins anew in May, and the buds of the trees start to sprout up, your love for me is making its presence known in all my hidden places taking, hold of my life.

Soon, it will be June, and the summer sun has come to melt down the remaining snow crust on the mountain's caps, giving the seedlings some much-needed water. Just as your love for me feeds my soul the nourishment it, needs to grow for you.

I'm telling you now that nothing stays the same forever, much like the leaves in Fall, which turn colors and start to fall. Your love for me has changed me in ways I have yet to discover.

Now, cold nights and secret affairs of winter have come with the chilly winds, snowballs, and freezing lakes, but your love for me keeps me warm inside.

Life is how we live it cold or warm, dark or bright, even when the clouds lurk in the sky. We shall play; we shall smile.

Yes, the season of change has come upon me with subtle beginning and the scent of a promise of change. I can feel something stirring inside me, and I have to ask, "will it be hopefulness, gratitude, openness, love, loss, or pain?" I will not know the answer to that question until change has completed its cycle within me, but whatever the answer is, it will be welcome into my life.

Miracles do happen that's All I Know

All I know is that I have loved you from the very first time we met. All I know is that while I was waiting for you to come back to me, I must have died thousands of times.

All I know is that I love the feeling I experience when you are by my side. I know that I'm the happiest I could be when I am greeted by you just like you greet the night as an old friend.

All I know is that I can never hide from you and pretend all is okay because you can always see right through me.

All I know is that if I had known then how you would change my life for the better, I would have never had any doubts.

All I know is that when I see you smile, all my troubles seem to vanish; my whole day is made better. Then, I know that miracles really do happen when I am with you!

Out of the Darkness & Into the Light

Open the window of your heart and let the love I have for you enter. Don't keep the love I have for you from shining into your life; draw back those curtains that keep you in the darkness.

Don't close me out from your life, let me come to you and bring you out of the darkness and into a new life. What I offer you will fulfill all your needs, because what I have to offer you is more than you could ever imagine.

Can't you hear me calling your name? Can't you hear me pleading for you to come to me?

Don't you know that I can hear the loneliness of your heart crying in the darkness? So come to me and let me lift you out of that darkness, and stand you in the light of my love.

To my Dad

There is so much I wish I could have told you (while I was with you).

First, I want you to know that you are my greatest hero. You are the strongest, most caring, most dependable, and the most honorable man I have ever known.

Thank you for always being there for me when I needed you the most. Thank you for providing a safe and healthy home for me. Thank you for the moral teachings and guidance you have instilled in me.

Most of all I want to thank you for showing me the love I needed the most, and for setting my feet on a path of meaning. I want you to know that all the lessons you have taught me have not gone to waste because I have taught them to my children.

These words only express a fraction of what is on my mind and heart; once again, thank you so much for all you have done for me.

Your loving child!

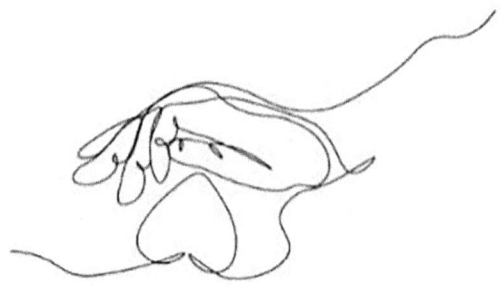

Oh my Love

Oh, my love, don't you know that when I found you I found someone who chose to stay even when I was an unlovable mess?

Oh, my love, don't you know that there must have been something in the air the day we met because all I could hear was the distant drums of my heartbeat pounding in my ears?

Oh, my love, don't you know that from the first time I looked into your eyes it was like looking into the cloudless night sky?

Oh, my love, how could I not have seen you standing right in front of me when you were standing there shimmering like the moonlight shimmers across the surface of the lake?

Oh, my love, don't you know that through all the heartbreaks, triumphs, trials, adventures, and moonlight walks on the beach, my life would not have been fulfilled?

The Myth

True love has always felt like a myth to me until my eyes met yours, and then I found the love of my life in you, my angel.

You always make me feel so safe and loved when I'm lying in your arms listening to your heartbeat, and as I wake up every morning I know that deep down my angel has watched over me throughout the night.

You always comfort me when I'm sad, and you have always wiped all my tear drops away. Oh my, the angel, I owe all my happiness to you, so thank you for never leaving my side, and thank you for being my angel every morning.

Inspired by Abigail Keen

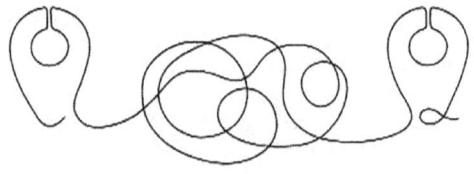

The Pathfinder

"This is the way," the Pathfinder called out. "I will guide you on the safe path; you only need to trust in me."

"Come with me," the Pathfinder called out, "and trust in me for I will guide you true and straight."

"Follow me," the Pathfinder called out, "follow my banner for it will never mislead you. If you only look up you will see it waving in the sky so noble and proud for all to see."

"Listen for my voice," the Pathfinder called out, "and follow my instructions, for I will never lead you into danger for My path is always true."

"Seek out the path I have laid before you," called the Pathfinder for my path is the only true path and all others will lead you into distraction.

Rally all to my banner, the Pathfinder said, so that all will follow the true path. Make my words become your words, my path become your path, and my light become your light. Become leaders of all mankind so they will not be lost for all time.

Know this and keep it in your heart as I am your Pathfinder and listen to my voice and follow my path, seek my banner, and will be treated as one of my children.

Beware of those who would lead you down the path of destruction but my path the true path will lead you into the light.

If you fail to heed the words of this Pathfinder you will fall into a world of darkness, a world of loneliness that you have never experienced before, and a world of your own making. And they will have to live in that world forever.

If you choose me to be your Pathfinder I will always guide you on the path of light, truth, and life. You will never have a doubt that the path I have chosen for you is the only true path.

God of Wonders

Above the sound of the crashing waves of the ocean, and above the sound of the thunder of the biggest storms, and above all the noise and confusion you have heard the whisper of my heart calling out for you.

I have always thought that you were just like the stars in the heavens, oh so beautiful to look at but just out of my reach. I have always known that I was not worthy of your love for me, which makes me try that much harder so I can feel worthy of just looking into your eyes.

When I needed you the most I knew where to look and it wasn't in the beauty of the rising sun, or the colors of a rainbow after a storm, or was it in the sight of the stars of a clear night sky. The place I needed to look was in that small quiet place deep inside of myself the place where I would humble myself upon my knees in prayer before you.

Oh God of wonders, You have always heard my prayers, and You have always led me to the place where you dwell.
Oh, my Lord God You have led me to the place of hope, love, and forgiveness. You have led me to my home to live with you forever and forever.

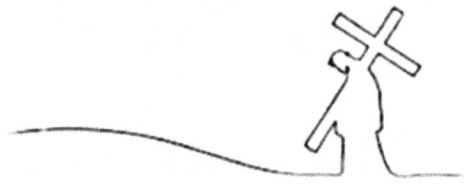

Oh Lord my God

I pray to you oh, Lord my God, to strengthen me with your sword and shield to let me see the vision you have for my life.

I pray to you oh, Lord my God, to live a life that is pleasing to your sight. I pray that I will one day stand in your presence and not be ashamed.

I pray to you oh, Lord my God, that I will honor all the blessings you have bestowed upon me. I pray for you to guide every footstep that I take, and to light the path that lies before me so that I may not stumble.

I pray to you oh, Lord my God, that with your guiding hand, I will overcome all of today's trials.

I pray to you oh, Lord my God, that riches I heed not, nor vain, empty praise. I pray the inheritance you have given me will not go to waste. And I pray to you Oh, High King of heaven, that the victories I won with your help may reach heaven and joys.

I pray to you oh, Lord my God, that you will be the heart of my own heart, that whatever may befall me I heed your call. I pray that you will always be my vision, oh ruler of my heart, I pray all this and more to you oh ruler of my life, ruler my soul, and ruler over all of creation.

Your Prayers

God has answered your prayers today and I am back in His arms again all because of your prayers. Thank you for praying, praying for me. I am where I am today all because of your prayers for me. Lord give me that heart of prayer today, so that I might restore others into your arms today.

From that simple prayer reminds me that in asking for these magnificent blessings I am also responsible to exhibit them to others. May others see His likeness reflected in my own life through those prayers.

How can I ever thank you for praying, praying for me? May

God bless you, and those you pray for this day.

I Can only Imagine

Is it my imagination or can I see all the wonders of God's creation when I look into your eyes?

Is it my imagination or can I hear angels singing when you speak?

Is it my imagination or can I feel the very presence of God when you are near me?

Is it my imagination or does it you can carry all my troubles away when I'm in your strong arms?

Is it my imagination or does time seem to stop when we are together?

Oh, my love, the answer to those questions and more is that it's not my imagination but true. For you have become the center of my life, and my whole world revolves around you.

God's Love for You

Kings and kingdoms will all pass away but God's love for you will only continue to grow and never fade away. Oh yes, the sun in the heavens and the stars too will all go out before His love for you fades away.

If you let God's love for you in, it will set your heart on fire, and oh yes how His love for you will burn deep in your soul.

I encourage you to take refuge in His loving arms and let the peace you find there rekindle the fire within your heart.

The Gift

I have seen you wandering in the darkness, and I have seen you searching all that was before you.

I have felt the heartache and misery that you endure, and I have felt the loneliness that dwells in your soul. And that is why I have given you a gift.

Oh, can't you see the gift I have left at your feet? Will you accept this gift of love, hope, and light that I have given you, or will you choose to stay in the darkness?

I can put an end to all your searching and wandering. I can put an end to all the heartache and misery that is in your life. All you have to do is accept this gift I now offer you.

I will take you through the darkness and chase all the shadows away, and all you have to do is accept my gift.

Mother's Prayers

Mom, God has answered your prayers today because I am back in His arms again all because of your prayers. Thank you for praying, praying for me. I am where I am today all because of your prayers for me. Lord give me that heart of my mother so that I may pray like her.

May my prayers restore others into your arms today as my mother's restored mine.

Those simple prayers remind me that in asking for these magnificent blessings I am also responsible to exhibit them to others. May others see His likeness reflected in my own life through those prayers.

How can I ever thank you for praying, praying for me Mom? May

God bless you, and all those you pray for.

Be Thou my Vision

When I invited you into my life, I felt like I had just woken up from a long winter nap. You came to me like the summer winds, so warm and refreshing. I welcomed you with open arms.

Let us wrap our arms around each other and guard each other from the darkness that surrounds us.

I was so fragile and weak before you came into my life, but your love and words strengthened me. You made all my troubles vanish into thin air.

The love I found in you was endless. Because of your love for me, I am so much more now than I was before.

Dear Reader:
This poem came to me in the dead of night, it came to me as if it was alive within me and full of colors. I had a hard time putting pen to paper what I saw in my mind. What I am trying here is to describe the feelings, sights, and colors of words I saw there that long night of writing. To this day I am not sure I have conveyed it the way I saw it. This is why I named it this way.

The River of Love

The love I have for you is like a waterfall and it flows out of me as a river flows over a cliff, and you can feel the power of my love for you if you stand on the banks of the river.

Oh, come to me and drink from the river of love I have for you and let the endless amount of love that flows there quench your soul.

Oh, come and listen for the thunder of my voice calling for you in the crashing water of that waterfall. Oh, come and rest by the still waters, and let my presence bring peace to your troubled mind.

So, come and let my love for you bring new life to you, just as the river gives new life to all that live on its banks.

Better Now

I am better now that you have come into my life because everything seemed to be over my head, Oh, how I would often stumble and fall on my face, only to find you by my side.

I am better now because you have thrown me a lifeline and rescued me from a dark and bitter life.

I am better now that I have come to you and humbled myself before you. Oh, how I felt so afraid to look into your loving eyes because I knew I was unworthy of the forgiveness that was within them.

I am better now that you have lifted me to my head off the ground and planted my feet firmly on the ground.

I am better now that you have shown me what I was made to be. And that is **<u>YOUR LOVING CHILD.</u>**

Somewhere over the Horizon

Somewhere over the horizon, I can see that there is a light, oh my love I know that you're waiting for me just over that horizon.

Though I may not know where this road may lead me I'll just keep walking down it with all my hope and faithfulness trusting that You'll be there when I get there.

Even though some days are still a mystery to me, I believe that in time the answers will be revealed to me. Even when the path is just not clear before me I know that somewhere over the horizon you are waiting for me

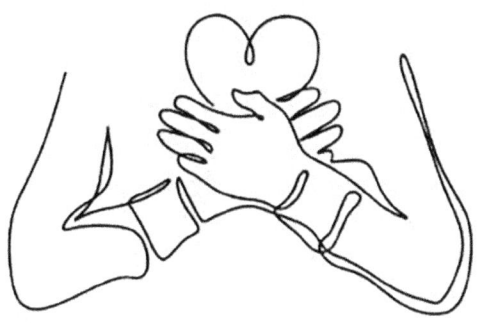

Deep Love

My love for you is so deep for you that it touches the very depths of my soul. It is a love that grows stronger with each passing day.

I can't picture anyone else as my lover. You make every single moment of my life more beautiful than the last. I couldn't be more grateful to have someone like you in my life. You have brought so much joy and happiness into my life.

Seeing the smile on your face makes me so happy to be alive. You are more beautiful than the sunset to me when I see you smile.

Knowing that I will spend the rest of my life with you has brought the greatest gift into my life.

Inspired by Abigail Keen

Undying Love

When you are near me I always feel the good vibrations that come from you, but when you're far from me it's hard for me to even carry on.

When we are close you have this way of making me feel alive, but when we are apart I feel dead inside. Oh, how I wish I understood these feelings I now have.

It's as if my heart is made of glass so vulnerable and weak. I fear that if I go too far away from you, it would shatter at any moment.

I want you to never forget that I truly love you and that sometimes it's hard for me to find words to tell you how much you mean to me.

I want you to understand that the Love I have for you will never change and that as each day goes by the love I have for you will grow until I take my last breath.

A Future Together

Years from now, our past will be a story; a story of long days and lonely nights, hard work, and lack of sleep.

We all live each day having intimately known the pain of being apart, we all appreciate and embrace our time together, knowing how lucky we are to have made it through, and we will find solace in the promise of a future together.

Step by Step

I have to admit that I no longer can fight these feelings I have for you. It has been so long that I had almost forgotten what it is like to love someone.

I thought that the love that was inside of me was so tainted that there was no hope for it. But step by step we have taken this fantastic, and wonderful journey together. We each have shared heartache and happiness. We have inspired and motivated each other to achieve goals that we would normally hesitate to dream of.

This Thing called Love

In my life, I have received the wonderful opportunity to experience the greatest emotion known to man and that emotion would be true love.

Now I know that love comes in many forms, and we love people in different ways and for different reasons, depending on how they have touched our lives.

I also know that love is a very powerful word and can describe a multitude of feelings, but its main context carries the same meaning.

But here in this context, I'm talking about that kind of love that you may only find once in your life, the kind of love that fits into the other half of your soul that has been missing.

I now must tell you that I'm very grateful to you for helping me find this happiness within myself. And for this reason, you have become the most important person in my life.

Not with Me

When you are not with me, you leave a hole in my heart so big that others can see it for miles away.

When you are not with me, you take away my sun and put it behind rain-filled clouds and that makes my day very gloomy.

When you are not with me, I feel like there is nobody left in this world to hold me tight, and that there is nobody left in this world to kiss me goodnight.

When you are not with me, your burning light that guides me is so faint that the darkness all but claims my soul.

Oh, my love come back to me and refill my life with your warming rays of love. Bring back to me the sun-filled days of my life that we shared once again, and bring back the smile on my face.

Searching the Horizon

As I stand at my window my eyes take in all the wonders God has to offer me this day, and I find that my mind is not content with what I see before me. I find that my eyes are searching for one thing that is missing from my life, and that is you.

As my eyes search the horizon for you, I have to wonder how others cope with the weight that they must bear. How do others deal with the hunger that lies within their very soul? How do they stop the heavy feeling of the worlds weight crushing them?

The loneliness, coldness, and fear grip me while I search the horizon, and I can't fight those feelings so I look inward to see the memories, photos, and texts that we have exchanged with each other so I can find peace and happiness once again!

I will not stop searching the horizon for you until I see you coming back to me.

A New Life

The very first time I met you and held you in my hands, I said to myself "Here begins a new life", and while I held your little body I could not but fall in love with you.

The first time I looked upon your angelic face I knew that here was the being of discovering toasting marshmallows over on open fire, sunrises and sunsets, days at the beach, and a day with friends.

As I stand here looking into your sleeping face you make me believe in angels and I see all of the adventures that the future holds for you. And as your little hand holds on to my finger my heart quickens.

I take in this sight before and quickly kiss your forehead and whisper into your ear "Sleep my angel and know you are loved!"

To Father

As I get older, I find that I have been asking this question a lot lately, "Where are those happy days of my youth?" To me, it seems that these times are so hard to find in today's world.

I look back and remember the time that I sat in my father's lap and he made me feel so loved and safe. I remember the times we played outside together.

Oh, how I remember those long talks we used to have where he always made me feel so wanted. I remember my father making time for me whenever I needed him.

Dad, I want you to know that the words "THANK YOU" will never express the gratitude that I have for you. Nor will a simple hug ever show you how much love I have for you.

As you sit here today and read these words, I want you to know that all sacrifices that you have made for me have not gone in vain. And nothing you have taught me was wasted for I now teach it to my children, and they will teach it to theirs.
So, Dad, these simple words will have to show you just how grateful I am.

Dad, I love you, and thank you for it all!

Daybreak

Daybreak has come once again, and the moon is quickly disappearing over the horizon. It is slowly giving up its claim to darkness and surrendering itself to the warming presence of the sun.

With the coming morning, I have found myself asking God that He would let me wake up next to you, to wander through the city with your hand in mine, and to let this day last as long as possible. So that I'll be happy for the rest of my life.

Changed My Life

In my lifetime, I have seen beauty and I have seen ugliness.

Oh, how I wanted to live in a dream world where I could just shut out all the ugliness and pain in this world and live in a world of love and acceptance.

I wanted to live in a world where I never worry about today because tomorrow brings new promises. A world where love is so pure that its light can be seen for miles.

But then, you came into my life and changed the world around me. You changed it into something that I never expected it was a world of new life, new hopes, and new meaning.

You changed my dream world into a world of reality.

To my True Love

I may not get to see or hear from you as often as you like, and I may stay away from your side for way too long. I also may not get to hold you in my arms all through the night.

I also want you to know that I can't and will never let you go, for you are embedded into my very soul. Oh, my love, I want you to consider these words as one big hug from me.

Oh, my love, when you are alone about to fall asleep at night I want you to remember me whispering into your ear, "Good night my love, and sleep tight!" and know that I'll be with you all through the night.

Hold fast to those memories for they will sustain you for the rest of your life. And you can rest free knowing that deep in my heart that you are the one and only one that I love!

From your true love.

The Depth of Love

Let me tell you about how I lose myself every time I look deep into your Angelic eyes, and about how you always seem to find me and take me to paradise.

Let me tell you about how I will kiss the top of your head, and whisper into your ear that you are loved and wanted.

Let me tell you about the eternal flame that you have ignited deep within my soul.

Let me tell you about how when you are in my arms all my doubts seem to vanish.

Oh, please let me tell of all these things, and let them be a reminder that my love for you comes in all these forms.

Inspired by Abigail Keen

Dreamed a Dream

I dreamed a dream and I was troubled by what I had dreamed.

In my dream, I saw you sitting by the cliff side and you were watching the horizon, but when I approached you I could see that you had been crying, and my heart melted at the sight that was before me.

My first thought was to rush into your arms and comfort you to take all your tears away. But I knew that this was just a dream and I knew deep down couldn't do anything for you.

I needed to know if you were rejoicing or if you were saddened for some unknown reason.

But what I saw next disturbed me the most. Because the sight before me started to fade so I started to run so I could hold you. But before I could reach you the sight of you was gone.

This woke me from my slumber and when my eyes opened my heart rejoiced at the sight you of lying next to me.

A New Song

What has happened to you, my love? You used to live on the edge of tomorrow with happiness and a song in your heart.

But something has happened to you and you no longer have that light in your eyes or that bounce in your step.

Oh, my love it breaks my heart to see you like this; will you please talk to me and tell me what has taken all your happiness away?

Oh, my love come to me, and let my love for you give you a new song, and let this new song fill your soul so that you may dance once again as you did before.

Oh, my love if you only come to me and cry on my shoulder, because I know that we can work this out so that you can live once more as you did before.

Don't let these chains of sorrow hold you down just come back to my loving arms where you belong!

Message of Love

My dear love know that you are the source of my courage, and you are the motivator I have always been looking for.

My love without you around, I often wonder how I will handle the adversities that lie before me.

My love when I think of you my world changes, and my heart bubbles with gladness. All my troubles seems to vanish and nothing seem to matter to me because you have lifted all my problems off from my shoulders.

My love know that I can't take my mind off you and that you are loved and honored in my life. You are everything to me, you bring out the best in me, and you are the one I want to share everything with (my thoughts, hopes, and dreams).

My love, you are such a source of inspiration for me, and I will forever be indebted to you for all you have brought to my life. So, to repay you, I promise you my heart and all the love in it for the rest of my life.

Inspired by Abigail Keen

To my Wife

A lot of times it's hard for me to tell you just how much you mean to me.

So, let me tell you about this new hunger that now resides within my soul. About this eternal flame that you have ignited deep within me.

I need you to understand that the love I have for you will never change, and as each day goes by the love, I have for you has grown and blossomed into something more powerful than the day before.

Please never forget that I LOVE YOU. And that I will love you forever and always until I draw my last breath.

Your Loving Husband.

Lonely Heart

Oh, my love, I need you to look deep inside your heart, and into the very depths of your soul then tell me what you feel. Because when I look into your eyes all I see is sadness.

Oh, my love, I can hear your lonely heart calling out my name. Your lonely heart is waiting for me to reduce you from all your loneliness.

Because I know I have searched the very depths of my being and I found more than enough love, and happiness to lift you out of any burden that may be weighing on your soul.

Oh, my love, take refuge within me and let my love for you fill you with it.

My Greatest Wish

I must praise the Lord above for sending you into my life. Because You're all that I've ever wished for.

All my life I prayed for someone like you and I have discovered that I will never find another person sweater than you, or one more precious than you.

At times it seems that You're all that I've ever known. And it makes me so happy when you smile because your face always seems to glow.

Oh, how you have turned my life around. Oh, do not look away from me, my love. I only ask that you set your eyes upon me as I prove to you how much you mean to me.

I will tell you now that I will cherish every hug, every conversation, every kiss, and every moment we have together.

Searching for you

I just want you to close your eyes and think of me in your heart where I can stay forever.

Don't you know that I have searched the world to find a person like you? And when the rain was pouring down, and my heart was hurting I kept looking but I didn't let anything stop me from making my dreams come true.

Let me tell you that after all the things we have said and done to each, other it has made my heart feel happier and fuller than ever before. So, I can tell you right now that no one will stand in the way of how I'm feeling for you.

I know people will try to divide what we have made together because they will not believe that what we have got is real. But I'm telling you right now that 'til the end of time, there ain't going to be no one who will separate us.

Good Morning my Love

I met you in my dreams last night and mmm what a dream. The love I feel for you is getting stronger. My head stays in the clouds as I go through the day with you always on my mind. I have a comforting feeling inside as well as that wonderful feeling of knowing that you love me. I pray that God will lead us where he wants us to be and through His eternal love our love will grow into a blessed life.

I know that the Lord above works in mysterious ways, and I feel that through Him this is what we have come to be.

I never thought that I could love someone as much as I love you. I know it's crazy but it's true. I do love you my special Sunshine.

I will always be here for you with a bigger share of my day, so have a beautiful day my love. Cherish each and every second.

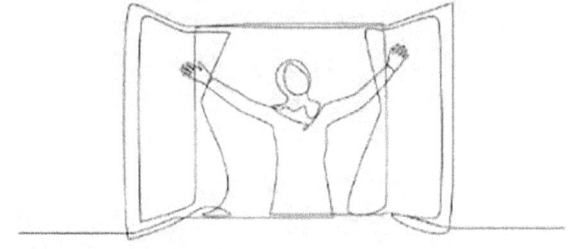

Loving you openly

Right now, you have eternity before you, and everything seems to be possible and attainable.

The real dangers of this world are unimaginable. I wish I could save you from them all, but some things can't be changed.

Let yourself love, and make sure you say the words. Don't hide from your feelings or keep them a secret. People may know you care, but they long to hear it. Don't keep them waiting.

Your heart will melt into another, and that love will transform you into your best self. Nothing will ever feel better.

Unfortunately, that connection will be devastatingly short. Pursue it anyway.

Immerse yourself in every moment. Stop and engage all your senses — see, hear, smell, feel, and taste all that you can. Fully experience every second.

Those memories will be your greatest treasures. Inspired

by Abigail Keen

My Dearest:

You are a surprising breath of fresh air. With each day you continue to influence my life. I thank you for all the support and kindness you have shown me. I truly have been blessed by God this day, for he has chosen you to guide me back into life. Take it to your heart and know that your message has been received read and cherished. I know from now on that I will forever be loved by you. And I hold that close to my soul.

You have become more to me in these last few weeks than I could ever ask for.

Yours always.

Limitless Love

Can't you hear the distant voices telling you to listen to your heart? Can't you hear my heart crying out to you? Because I've been calling you by name to come to me, and if you listen to the wind that carries my voice on it you can hear me there.

Can't you feel the tears I have shed for you in the rain that falls on your head? Don't you know that once the rain stops and has washed all the suffering away it feels like the rainbows in the sky?

Can't you see the love I have for you is like that of a sleeping child? And don't you know that my love for you transcends the darkest night, the highest mountain, and even the stars themselves?

Can't you tell that when I am with you, all time stops. And don't you know that I am and always will be with you.

From the Northern winds, the rainfall, the rainbows in the sky, the peace of a sleeping child to even time itself I have shown you the love I have for you.

Always and forever yours.

My little Moon Shadow

Oh, my little Moon Shadow you have given me the courage to live in this dark world.

Oh, my little Moon Shadow your love has found me, and it's the greatest feeling I have ever had.

Oh, my little Moon Shadow your love for me is like the stars in the sky lighting up the darkest night. And that chain of light will guide me for the rest of my life.

Oh, my little Moon Shadow at last, I can call you my own and when you are gone from my side It's like you take the sunshine with you.

Moon Shadow as long as I have you I'm home!

Mom & Dad

Just knowing that we have given you a lifetime of memories, joys and dreams. Has made us into the source of your pride and happiness. For your golden memories has become our wealth.

Every Night

Every night, I gladly give up my heavenly paradise just so I can spend a little time with you even if just in your dreams.

Every night, I come to you and whisper into your ear of the love I have for you.

Every night, our souls intertwine once again, and speak that undying love for each other.

Every night, my arms reach out to hold you with every ray of light from the star above your head.

So, sleep tight this night and know that I hold you in my loving arms, and can you be at peace for you are safe here in my arms.

The River of Love

The love I have for you is like a waterfall and it flows out of me as a river flows over a cliff, and you can feel the power of my love for you if you stand on the banks of the river.

Oh, come to me and drink from the river of love I have for you and let the endless amount of love that flows there quench your soul.

Oh, come and listen to the thunder of my voice calling for you in the crashing water of that waterfall. Oh, come and rest by the still waters, and let my presence bring peace to your troubled mind.

So, come and let my love for you bring new life to you, just as the river gives new life to all that live on its banks.

I Will Walk with You

I will walk with you by the light of the silvery moon, and never leave you in the dark!

I will you walk with you 'till all the stars have all been blown out, and there is no more sunrises, or sunsets left!

I will walk with you 'till I can't hear your heartbeat anymore, and till every sound stops and silence cries out to be heard!

I will walk with you 'till I live within the shadow of your heart!

I will walk with you 'till time stops and has no meaning anymore!

Yesterday

How I long for yesterday; how I long for the days of old. I hold fast to those old times because of what I see in my mind.

In my mind I still can see you as you were when we first met, I can still see you walking on the beach next to me, and I still see you lying on the floor in front of the open fire.

Oh, how time has slipped through my fingers and all those old times are gone. But I am glad that together we were able to chase our dreams into the ground and made each day count.

And I am glad that in this lifetime I was able to meet my special soul, who was able to fill my very essence with an almost overflowing cup of friendship.

Just so you know the soul and the love there in is embedded so deep in my heart now that no matter where you go, whether it be in this life or another, my soul is sure to follow because no distance can put out its flame.

By Loving Me

By loving me, I hope you find the freedom to be all you hope for, and I hope you find the home you desire.

By loving me, I just hope that you find that I will never let you go and that I could never move on if you left me.

By loving me, I hope you find that I will follow you anywhere you ask me to and that I would do anything you may ask me to do just to make you smile.

By loving me, I hope you find the life that you have always dreamed of, and I hope you find the peace you long for.

By loving me, I hope that I am at your side when you find these things and that you have chosen me to make all these things come true with you.

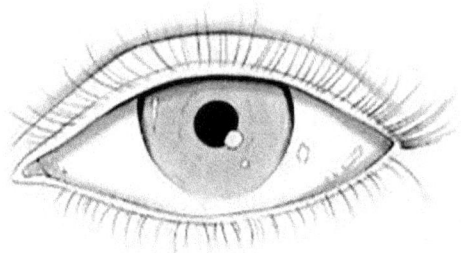

From the First Look

From the first time, I looked into your eyes, I became your willing victim, and from that first look, you took my heart hostage.

From the first time, I looked into your eyes, I knew that I had found the other half of my soul, and from that first look, I knew I would be yours forever.

From the first time, I looked into your eyes I knew that I'd never be alone again, and from that first look, all time seemed to stop.

From the first time, I looked into your eyes I knew my life would never be the same, and from that first look the chains from around my heart fell away.

It only took one look from you and I knew that my life of loneliness had come to an end.

Bound in Love

Standing here, I see every dream the Lord has for me is bound in love.

Every longing in my heart brings me a little closer to the place I need to be, and that is with my Lord Jesus Christ.

As He watches me grow daily bound in his glory, I reach for all He desires.

Everything I want to be, everything I long to be, and everything I dream to be is bound in God's love.

A Morning like No Other

Arise, arise, and greet the day for it's a beautiful morning. Oh, can't you see that God has made this day just for you?

Jump up and get ready for the day is waiting for you to come and play. Make yourself ready for the best part of the day is waiting.

Oh, do be quick or you will miss the painted sky that God has made, and do bring your favorite chair with something hot to drink so that you can truly enjoy all that He has made for you today.

Please don't forget your Bible so that you can get your mind, heart, and soul in tune with what God has for you this day.

Have a wonderful day!

My Dearest Loving Husband

Oh, my love, it's a beautiful morning and it was created for your happiness and joy. So, my love, I leave you a message this day; it is a message of how my heart sings of your praises and the love I have for you.

Oh, my love, I love how you make me want to wake up each day from my slumber, and the feeling of staying up late at night exchanging sweet words with you.

Oh, my love, I hope this message pierces through your heart and enables you to understand the words that I speak.

Oh, my love, I know that I may not be able to send you the perfect message of love every hour, or even every second of the day. I want you to know that you are the breath I take, and the fire that rages in my heart. So, my love I want you to enjoy the wonders of this day and take comfort in the fact that you are very dear to me, and that you are loved.

Your Loving Wife.

My Love for You

I see you in my thoughts and dreams, and when I awaken, I think of how real it all seemed. Then I remember that you are not here to comfort me or hold me, but in my heart, I know that you will be back with me soon.

I know that inside the walls of your heart, you are doing time, because by not being here with me you punish yourself for the crime of loneliness.

I want you to know that others in your life will come and go, but my love for you is true, and I'm sure you know it. You also know that you have my heart in your hands and that my love for you is what you truly own. So, come back soon and make our house a home.

When you go to sleep this night take this to heart you are my stars, my moon, and my sun. And when you're gone from my side it's like someone came and took all my happiness away.

Oh, my love can't you see that I love you so much that it's hard for me to breathe when you're gone like this?

Inspired by Abigail Keen

Words from Your Lips

I want to know how the words "I love you" sound like when they come from your lips. I want to know what it feels like to have your finger touch my face.

I want to know what it would be like to hold you in my arms. I want to know what it would be like to share a moonlit stroll along the beach with you.

But I never want to know the feeling of you not in my life, and I never want to know what it would be like to be not loved by you.

Oh, my love even though I can't hear your words right now, or feel your body next to mine, I want you to know that you are the very breath I take. You are loved more than you can ever imagine.

Longing for You

I look up at the stars and think of you tonight; wishing I could see their light reflecting in your eyes.

How I long to touch you, and hold your body close to mine. As we share our love beneath the perfect sky this very night.

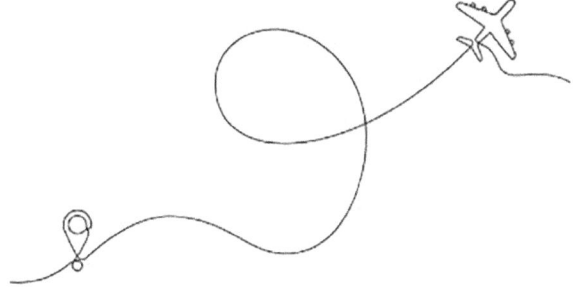

Daily Journeys

Even though my daily journeys are filled with trials and triumphs the Word of the Lord guides my feet.

When I feel incomplete, unfinished, or distressed I build and strengthen my fortress upon the Word of the Lord.

Let Go of the Past

I'm telling you now that there are memories right now that you're afraid to face. The terrible things that you have imagined and the real memories of what did happen.

I'm telling you that the only way you will ever put the coming hell behind you is to go through it. And by throwing your fears aside and facing each monster head-on.

By doing this you will not only conquer your demons, but you will conquer your past. Then it won't be long before they have no hold over you.

Now once you have let your past go, it will not continue to control your life, and you'll be ready to be a guide to others as they learn how to heal from their pain from you.

This will be excruciating to you, and you will cry — a lot — but you'll also heal.

Inspired by Abigail Keen

How to Measure a Person Worth

The ultimate measure of a person cannot be found when you look at where they stand in the moments of comfort and convenience, but where they stand at times of challenge and controversy.

If you want to see the true measure of a person, watch how they treat their inferiors, not their equals. The true measure of a person is how they treat someone who can do them no good.

If there is any truer measure of a person then is not by what they do, but by what they give back to mankind.

The measure of a person is what they do with the power they hold. Because a strong person gets up, but a stronger person gets up for others.

Idea of Freedom

A great warrior is not made by the weapons they carry, the horses that they ride, or even the men they command. A great warrior lets no chain of anger, hatred, or opposition hold him.

A great man humbles himself before the world, but he stands fast to his godly morals, and his God-given right to live free.

A great man not only keeps himself free from the chains of slavery but shows others how to free themselves as well. A great man sees that his strength comes from his mind and not the weapons he holds.

Loving You

It has come to my attention that it's time to come to a major decision in my life about how I feel about you. Because you have made it clear that our relationship is at a turning point.

You see up to this point in my life I have never given my feelings much thought. But you have changed that, and you have made me feel things that I thought were long buried.

Now there have been times in my life when nothing happened, and I have noticed that it is in the quietness of these times that my soul expands. I now find myself in one of those times and I long for my soul to expand.

Can I truly say "**I LOVE YOU**" without asking myself why? Can I see a life without you in it? Can I stop thinking about you for two seconds? Will the person I'm seeing see who I am? Do I bear all my weaknesses? These are just some of the questions that run through my mind at this turning point.

So, when I tell you "I love you" take it to heart because it means a lot more to me than some fancy words. But also know that I don't take these words lightly. For I do not say these words as a father says them to a child; I also do not say these words as a husband may say then to his wife, but I say them as I would say them to myself.

Distant Light

When I was a younger man, I noticed this distant light that seemed to shine the brightest when I was on the path of destruction.

This distant light faded from time to time, but it was always there to guide me back home.

One day I was drawn far down the wrong path, so far that it was hard to see that light. It was then that light seemed to come alive getting brighter than I had ever seen it before.

It was then that out of the corner of my eye, I saw my mother praying as she had never prayed before, she was praying for me to come back to the Father.

Now that I'm back with the Father, that light is no longer distant, but it's alive within me brighter than ever.

My Father told me that if it wasn't for my mother's prayers, I wouldn't have seen that distant light.

That is why this is all I can say **"Thank you, Lord, and I am thankful that my mother gave her time in prayer. Thank you so much MOM, I love you"**.

Your loving son.

Your Touch

Don't you know that I thirst for you and that I have a desire to hold you every second of my life? That your touch leaves an imprint on my skin with a drowning need for you?

Don't you know that I wait for you to reach out to me with every breath I take and to take me into your arms and hold me forever? All I want is to look upwards with you and share the wonders that we see there.

Don't you know that you light up my life every time you call? That out of a billion people in the world, I selected you, and that I only love you.

Christ in Me

As I drink from the water that flows out of my Savior; Christ continues to fulfill my every need.

Then through my daily journeys, I make Jesus my foundation in which I place my life in His hands.

I have found that all I need is God and time.

Hand in Hand

Oh, lift your head high and look toward the sky so that you can see that the love I have for you is a symphony of perfect harmony.

Have faith, and believe in me then give me your hand so that we can walk hand in hand through all eternity.

Oh, be not afraid, for I am with you all the while. Oh, can't you see that this is our destiny and that there is no greater love than I have for you, I will show you that love such as I have for you can exist beyond while walking hand in hand with me.

The Prayer

Since you are my rock and fortress for the sake of your name lead me and guide me.

Keep falsehood and lies far from me give me my daily bread. Otherwise, I may have too much and disown you and say, "Who is the Lord?"

Or I may become poor and steal and dishonor the name of God. I only ask for wisdom and understanding so that I may glorify God in my daily life.

Psalm 31:3; Proverbs 39:8,9

Feel My Love

Open your heart, and close your eyes, my love. Feel my love for you reach beyond the sky.

Be careful with me my love because right now I am feeling so small and afraid for I'm still learning how to love you.

Oh, please say something to me my love so that I know you're not giving up on me. Oh, please make my heart sing this day my love just by saying my name.

Inspired by Abigail Keen

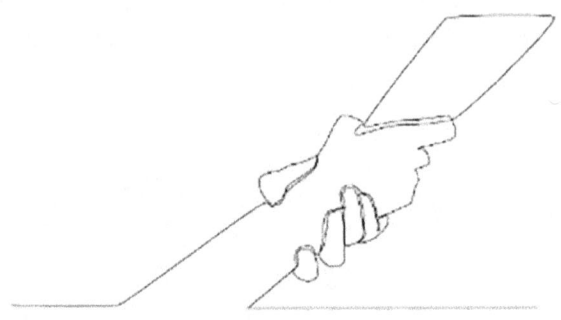

Trust in You

I have trust in you, for you are faithful and true.

With a touch of wisdom from you, I have realized that you're just a prayer away. You are my hiding place, and you are my salvation.

I lift my voice to heaven and sing your name, for you are my everything!

Magic of Love

Oh, can't you see what your love has done to me? Just look into my eyes and see the answer there. Please don't let the magic between us die.

Don't let this moment slip away because somewhere in the darkness true love waits for you, so don't be afraid of being hurt.

You must be brave now and believe that magic works. This is your final chance to hold the one you love.

Please don't hide your feelings for me on the inside, but know that this is just another turning point for us to take. I know you have waited long enough so reach out and take hold of my love for you.

Good morning Sweetheart!

Oh, my love; how the morning breeze on my face makes me think of you, the sun on my skin makes me think of you, and even the birds singing their beautiful songs make me think of you.

Oh, my love; we both knew our friendship would grow right from the very first day we spoke. But, neither one of us could begin to imagine the love we both would feel exploding and thundering into our hearts.

Oh, my love; our love is slowly growing into a beautiful relationship that only you and I can understand. We don't even need to be together, for we are never apart. You are my soulmate, my best friend, my inspiration, my love, and my all.

Hear These Words

As the sun rises over the horizon, it paints the sky in vivid colors, and I find that the only thing on my mind is you.

How can I ever compare your beauty to that which God had made for me this day? To me not only are you beautiful on the outside, but your inner self shows your compassion, your wisdom, your strength, and your commitment.

Just as God has honored me by showing me His power through the sunrise. You have honored me by showing me that you love me just by being here for me.

God may have lifted me out of the darkness and despair of life, but you (my love) have filled my life with new meaning. You have filled that void that God can't the void of true human Companionship!

I know I don't say it very often and I may not show you how I feel, but **_I do love you!_**

I pray that you hear these words because they come straight from my heart.

Your Presence

In the beginning, you were seated beside me in the night, by the lakeside.

And my hand was wrapped around yours like a crown.

I saw you smile when the air raised my hair in the breeze. Then you whispered into your ear; **"I love you more every day."** And for me, it was a touch of grace.

But all of a sudden, reality brought me back to where it began, in bed with your picture lying by my side.

You are beautiful.

Yes, that is what you are.

By Abigail Keen and Gene Johnston

The Darkness

Shunning the darkness, a bright light has emerged, marking the arrival of a new day known.

Open your eyes to a lovely morning that will fill your life with more love and happiness. May you find peace and joy today.

Have a fabulous day, my love.

Morning Comes

Morning has finally come, and each of us greets it differently. I for one have been blessed this day to realize that a special person has come into my life.

I employ you to take this moment to open your eyes and see that what we have made together is real. I want you to feel gratitude for the day that we will share. I am patiently awaiting what tomorrow has in store for us.

Take confidence to know that no distance can weaken the bond that we now share, and nothing can erase the memories from our minds.

I tell you now that our hearts will always be tied together, and from this moment on we will be of one mind, soul, and life.

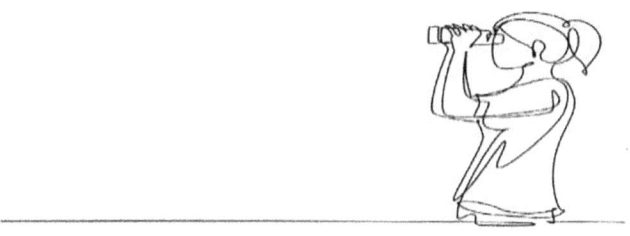

When I see you

When I look at you, I see heaven in your eyes, and I see underserved love for me.

When I see you stand before me, I see the stars in the sky, the vibrant colors of love, and I see my world may all my love.

So, tell me right now why should I look for another Moon or another Sun? Because what I see before me will always be enough for me.

One Love

Let it be known that I've chosen one person to love, one person to cherish, one person to protect and one person to stand up for.

That my arms will hold you when you are weak. My eyes will find you charming in your worst appearance, my heart will love you more even when you are most vulnerable.

That my love for you is like the oceans. Boundless, flowing, lively, beautiful, and endless. That I will be true to you when everybody walks away. And that I will love you from now till the end of time.

Inspired by Abigail Keen

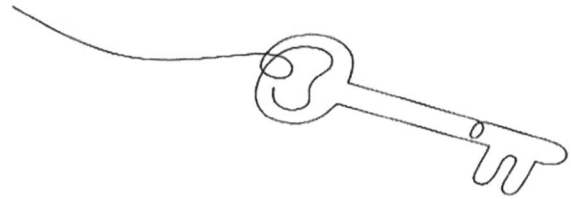

You are the Key

Oh, my love you are the key that opens my heart, and it is yours to explore from the inside, where you can pull on all my strings.

Don't you know that when I gaze into your eyes, I find that you make me feel complete, so let's stop time so it lasts forever?

Let me tell you right now that it seems like our love has no end and no beginning, and that we have been in love with each other forever.

Oh, let the choir sing to the world know that what we have together is real.

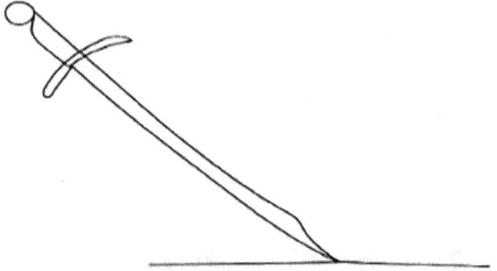

The Sword of the Lord

With the Sword of the Lord, we do battle with the unrighteousness, while standing on the foundation of the Word. We bring mercy and justice to those who defile the glory of God.

I lift up the Word in the darkness and the Word lights my path. With that Word, I slay all unrighteousness, and with that same Word, I bring the list out of the darkness and give hope to the world.

For I was lost in the darkness of death and was given the light of life.

To My Precious Angel

Ho, my precious child, I have found that the years have slipped away from me and you are no longer the child I once knew.

It was as if I just closed my eyes for but a moment and suddenly an adult stood where a child used to be. You should know that I may not carry you now in my arms but I will always carry you in my heart.

I want you to know that you have given me so many reasons to be proud of the person you have become, but the proudest moment for me is telling others that you are my child.

As I sit here reminiscing about the good times, we had I have to thank the good Lord above for giving you to me.

Forever & Always Mom

Bright Eyes

The first time I looked into those bright shiny eyes of yours, I saw such a passion for life that it frightened me. Because I knew deep down that a passion so pure, so consuming, and so perfect could not exist.

And yet, the longer I looked into those pools of living fire, the more I wanted to let myself fall.

Oh, how the desire to turn around and run was so great it almost overwhelmed me, but those bright loving eyes of you just drew me ever so close to you.

I often wonder; how a does poor boy like me talk to an Angel like you?

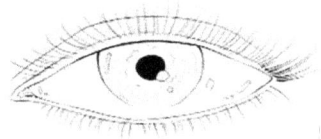

Your Eyes

All the wonders of the universe are revealed to me when I look into your eyes, I see all the stars above your head, I see the love you have for others, and I see the story of my life is written within them.

Oh, please let me rest my weary soul in the vastness of that love you have. Let me rewrite my life story so it may be pleasing to your eyes.

I have nothing to offer you but myself so please take this life and make it useful to all. Let this offering I now give you enough to be worthy of your love.

I must now thank you because whenever I look into your eyes, they have always made me feel wanted.

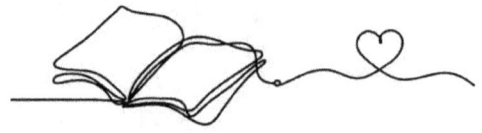

Stories of your Love

I hope the whole world hears the stories of how your love for me has saved me from a world of misery.

The story of how I gave you the key to open my broken heart, and of how you walked right in and made my heart all new.

The story of how I was on my knees in the darkest place of my life when I found you.

The story of how I stopped running from myself and walked right into your loving arms, and of how I no longer walk alone, of how I no longer stand alone, of how you have made my life whole.

I'm here to testify that my life would not be as rich, full, and complete without you.

Even when I let you see my scars you did not turn from me, and you did not send me away; you saw me as I was, and you still loved me enough to hold me in your arms.

Boundless Love

From the very instance, you came into my life, I knew that I had made the right choice. And from that point on I never had any doubts about your love for me because you showed me the true meaning of love.

With one little smile from you, people around you can feel the love flow out of you. I have witnessed the magic of your love transform lives right before my eyes.

Your perfect boundless love has lifted me into a new state of peace. I know that I will never hunger for the fake love I knew before you, and I know that your love is all I need to sustain and feed my soul.

You have been and always will be my rock, my salvation, my inspiration, and my comforter. You are the one from whom I have gained all my strength and become more than I could ever dream.

Counting my Blessings

As I lie here watching the moonlight dance across your face, I count all the blessings that I have received since you came into my life.

I have discovered that it was only because of your love for me that I was gifted with the most wonderful gift that I could have ever received.

As I lie there itching every inch of your face into my memory, I realize just how blessed I am.

As you lie there sleeping my love, take comfort that you are safe here in my loving arms.

I Take Comfort

Oh, how I pray that you hear my plea. Come to me and calm my soul; take from me the pain of loneliness and give me back the peace of mind I once had.

Don't you know that I take comfort in your words "I will always be here for you when you need me, and I will love you no matter what trials that may come into your life."

Can't you see how much I miss you when you're not with me? Can't you hear me crying in the darkness, and see me hoping for just one more day with you? Can't you feel how every fiber of my soul reaches out to you when you're gone from my side?

Don't you know that sometimes late at night if I'm very still I can hear your voice and your footsteps by my bed? Don't you know how much my heart yearns to hear those sounds when you are far from my side?

God of Wonders

Above the sound of the crashing waves of the ocean, and above the sound of the thunder of the biggest storms, and above all the noise and confusion you have heard the whisper of my heart calling out for you.

I have always thought that you were just like the stars in the heavens, oh so beautiful to look at but just out of my reach. I have always known that I was not worthy of your love for me, which makes me try that much harder so I can feel worthy of just looking into your eyes.

When I needed you the most I knew where to look and it wasn't in the beauty of the rising sun, or the colors of a rainbow after a storm, or was it in the sight of the stars of a clear night sky. The place I needed to look was in that small quiet place deep inside of myself, the place where I would humble myself upon my knees in prayer before you.

Oh God of wonders, You have always heard my prayers, and You have always led me to the place where you dwell. Oh, my Lord God You have led me to the place of hope, love, and forgiveness. You have led me to my home to live with you forever and forever.

My Little Angel

Oh, how I remember when I first lost my mind, it was the first time I held you in my arms and when I looked upon your sleeping face. Because at that moment everything I thought I knew seemed wrong, and my job in this world became clearer to me.

Oh, how I remember that first look. You were the most amazing thing that I have ever beheld. I had waited nine long months for this day to arrive but when you came to me all I could do was cry. You were so small and fragile I was so afraid for you and did not want to ever let you go.

Oh, hush now my angel there's no need for you to cry, I know it is a scary new world for you, but I will always be here for you. You will always have a hand to hold, a shoulder to cry on, open arms waiting for you, a loving family to support you, and a home to rest your head.

Oh, my little angel sleeps peacefully in my loving arms, and know that I will never let any harm befall you. Let the song I sing to you bring you comfort and joy.

Oh, my little angel let the love I have for you keep you warm throughout your entire life. Let the shelter that I have provided for you protect your entire life. Oh, my angel, it's a new dawn and a new day know that when you keep me by your side all will be okay.

This is for all those new mothers.

Inspired by Kloey Guerin

Look into my Eyes

When I look into your eyes, I find the world that I belong in. And I find myself in a world filled with love, hope, peace, and happiness.

When I talk to you, I find a person who can understand my deepest thoughts, and I find that I'm not all alone in this world.

When I listen to you, you help me hear the language of love, and I find that I can love that way too.

When I hold you, in my arms I find a world of acceptance. And I find that I've been transported into a world of unity.

When I make you number one in my heart, you become the center of my universe. And I find that all time stops, and you are the only person I need.

When I walk with you holding your hand watching the world speed past us, I find my life has become perfect. And I find myself wondering how I got so lucky to find an Angel like you.

My world has become the eyes that I look into every day, the voice I hear in my heart, the arms that hold me fast, the heart that beats in my soul, and the part of me that I will never let go. You are my ever-lasting companion, my hope, my light, my peace, my life, and my all. So, when I say **I LOVE YOU** I know you will hear me and hold me tight.

Power of Love

Don't underestimate what the power of my love for you can do because; I was able to cross the horizon to find you, and I was able to give you a place to rest within my heart.

Don't you know that the power of my love for you multiplies each and every day?

That it can outshine the darkest night, that it can rescue the most broken soul, and that it can lift **even you** out of the darkest times of your life?

Sending You My Love

My dearest love, I'm sending you all the love that you deserve in this bottle so that you can see it anytime you need to.

My dearest love, I know that deep down inside you are not only the one I want but you are the one I need.

My dearest love, if you place this bottle in any room, you are in it will light up the darkest corner and lift you out of any darkness that may visit you.

My dearest love, I'm sending this bottle so you can always hold it close to your heart, and let it warm your soul.

My dearest love, never open this bottle because if you do the love, I have stored there just for you will escape into the world and you will only be left with a small portion of my love.

My dearest love, carry this bottle at all times and let it give you hope, peace, light, and happiness in times when all seems lost.

made with love

The Love I have

Today, when I woke up, I noticed the one thing that I was sure of was that your face is the first and last thing that I want to see each and every day.

Now, I'm not sure where the love I now have for you started, or where my feelings I have for you changed so much.

But what I am sure of, is that the love I have for you is now stronger, deeper, and truer than I have ever thought possible.

Thinking of You

The memories we have shared and the adventures we have taken will always remain in my heart. No matter the distance we are apart, or the length of time we have spent without each other I can always count on those memories to ease the pain of missing you each day.

I take comfort in the fact that you are already just a thought away. Because if it was not for those memories of you, my world would fall apart. There is nothing more comforting to me than to have you so close to me.

Thank you for making these memories, and adventures possible, thank you for allowing me to find this kind of peace of mind. Thank you for showing me what true love was. Thank you for blessing me with these things and so much more!

Wayward Child

Oh, my Lord and God, I was a wayward child, and how I ran from you. I realize now just how wrong I was and how truly wicked I was.

Oh, my Lord and God, you poured your love and kindness into my life, and it was a love and kindness I did not deserve, and I rebelled against it.

You have shown me more mercy and grace than any one person should be shown, and I took advantage of it.

Oh, my Lord and God, you have offered me strength and protection in times of trouble, and I have told you that I could do it on my own.

You have always walked beside me and provided light for me to see by, and I chose to walk in the darkness.

Oh, my Lord and God, you have now shaped my life into a life of honor and joy you have created within me a new life; you have crafted a heart of love and a soul of understanding. You have made within me a never-ending fire to share your love with the entire world. You have made a way for this wayward child to come home to the inheritance that you have provided.

You are the One, the Lord, the All Mighty, the Giver of Life, the Great I Am. You have fulfilled all your promises to me by returning this wayward child to the place that I belong and that is by your side.

Yesterday, Today, & Tomorrow

Yesterday I was walking through this life as if it was a dream, and all I was doing was trying to stay alive. I was going nowhere fast and I had no idea what I was looking for. All my troubles were keeping me in the darkness of this world.

But today what I was seeking has come into view, and now see all of God's beauty around me, and I take into my soul to restore every fiber of my being.

Tomorrow with your guiding help will seek out and find the truth, beauty, love, and peace of all of your creation. With your love, I will become what you made me to be.

Your Magic

There's magic in your eyes because when I look into your eyes, I can see the love you have for me is real.

There's magic in your smile because when I see you smile it melts my heart, and warms all those around you.

There is magic in your touch because every time you touch me my heart skips a beat. And your touch has healed my broken heart.

There's magic in your voice because every time you speak my name, I fall in love with you all over again.

With your magic, you have created within me a never-ending fire of devotion, an open mind, a heart that sings of hope for my fellow man, and a life of humility, self-sacrifice, and symmetry. You have given me a life worth living. The magic you hold in your soul has made me believe in Angels.

You're the One

Before you, I was just walking through this life and I was just trying to stay alive. I was going nowhere and I had no idea what I was looking for.

But once I found you, you gave me a place within your soul to grow into the person you needed me the most.

Now that I am with you I know deep down inside my heart that you are not only the one I want to be with, but the one I need the most.

Upward and Onward

When hatred and destruction cross my path God shows me how to move upward and onward.

When pain and misery enter my life God once again shows me how to move upward and onward.

When all my worldly plans fall apart God once again shows me how to move upward and onward.

When my heart is broken and all my troubles are laid on His altar God lifts me and carries me home.

God has shown me how to move onward and upwards in all of life's battles.

If you let God, He will also show you how to move onward and upward and He will empower you to overcome all of life's trials.

I Hear Your Tender Whispers

The graceful words from your lips are like magic to me as they softly rise above the noise around me, and I hear the tender whispers and passionate cries of love you have for me.

Oh, how your mouth speaks fountains of life into my soul, and in the storms of my life you create within my life and not death by saying the simple words "**<u>You are loved</u>**".

When darkness nears, and my hope flickers you become that beacon of light in the darkest night that guides me through into gentle might.

I cherish this gift you have given me, and I will always hold it in my heart where I will let it grow, and dwell to give me the strength to carry on each and every day.

Life Fulfilled

Do you know what you do for me when you speak words of encouragement to me?

Do you know how I feel when I'm feeling down and I get a simple message from you asking how am I?

Do you know the weight of sadness, heartache, loneliness, and pain you lift off my shoulders when you just listen to me and show me that you care?

Do you know how much better my life has become with you in it with me?

Do you know how lucky I am to find a person like you?

Do you know how I feel when you come to me and sit with me and not say one word to me that is not damaging?

Do you know the light, joy, and peace of mind you bring into my life?

You are the one who has given my life meaning, purpose, and fulfillment. You have stood beside me in my darkest hours, you have given me your strength to hold on to when mine had faded. You have always encouraged me to believe in myself, you have inspired me to be better than others expect me to be, you have always kept me in mind when I was far from you, and you have always seen more in me than I see in myself. For this, all I have to give you is this simple poem that I have written just for you, and my deepest thanks and gratitude. **<u>Thank you so much for being you!</u>**

Only You

In the time we have been together, I found that it is only you that makes me smile, that it is only you that my eyes search for in a crowded room, and that it is only you that my heart yearns for every day.

Oh, my love, rest assured that it's your voice that I hear calling out to me in my dreams, and it's your touch that hunger for.

Oh, my love, look into my eyes and see the passion that burns therein for you. Lay your hand upon my chest and feel the heart that only beats for you.

Oh, my love, let me hold you so that I can feel the heat that radiates from your body, let me place my head upon your chest so that I can hear the heart the east therein, let me look into your eyes and see the fire that burns there, and let me quench my hunger for you with a kiss from your lips.

Oh, my love, hold on to me as we walk through this life so that we can show the world how to create a life of fulfillment. Let us show the world how to love and not hate. Let the words, **I love you let you** up and give you strength. Oh, my love, take comfort in the knowledge that you are and forever will be the only true love in my life.

Life with you

From the very first day we met you completely took my breath away. And from the first time I wrapped my arms around you, I thought that you were the most beautiful view I ever laid my eyes on.

To this day you look the same to me as if not one day has passed.

And oh, how I still carry the flame that keeps burning with the love I have for you in my heart.

Through all these years you've been by my side and walked hand and hand in happiness, wealth, sadness, loneliness, and poverty. We did all this with unconditional love for each other.

The love we have for each other has created a bond between the two of us, and nothing will ever break us apart. The radiating fire that is within our hearts keeps us warm in all we shall do and keeps us young at heart for each other.

For nothing the love that we have will change inside us we will always remain kindred souls until the day we're no longer able to carry on.

Without You

I now sit here thinking of you as the sun goes down for the day. I sit here wondering why you were taken away from me when we had so much more, to do.

For me, it seems that life never went as planned, or you'd still be right here with me locked, hand and hand in an embrace of our love, for eternity.

Instead, all alone I now must sit with only the thoughts of you in my mind. As I sit here, it doesn't do me any good to think about our lost love for my soul is now completely numb.

As I write you, these thoughts I can only hope that my words and thoughts are heard somewhere beyond this fallen sunset, and though our world has been stirred I haven't lost sight of the day when we first met.

Holding hands is how it first started and I tried to hold on 'till my dying day but my heart left when you departed, as I wanted for you to always stay with me.

My time left here is going to be tough knowing I must do it all alone. I must now draw on the knowledge, strength, and love I have gained from you to carry me through today and into tomorrow.

My only dream now is the day that you and I are reunited within the hands of the loving Father once more, and forever.

Miracles Do Happen

All I know, from the very first time I met you; I believed that the tales I heard about you seemed to be things of people's imagination and that those who faithfully followed you were out of their minds.

To me, it seemed that the stories that I heard of how people who followed Your footsteps were guided by some unknown force and that it was like you could see every unseen danger that lay before them.

To me, it seemed that the stories of your strength, resolve, and wisdom were beyond the understanding of my simple mind.

To me, it seemed that I was undeserving of anything you had to offer me, and I could not do anything to change how you saw me in your eyes.

Then you told me that all I had to do was, "Seek and I would find, ask and it would be given me, and knock and the door shall be opened unto you." "To all who are thirsty, I will give freely from the springs of the water of life."
Once I opened that door my eyes were opened, my mind was freed, and my life was transformed into a life of LIFE and not Death.

To my Beloved Sister

First off, I want you to know that all the prayers you have made for me have been heard and answered.

Second off, I may not say it often enough to you but I do love you, and I have prepared a special place in my heart just for you.

God has blessed you as has heard you. God has used you in ways you do not yet know.

I have seen the faith that you have in God your Father and I have seen the strength that he has given you to journey through this life.

Did you know that there were times in my life when God chose you to show me how to tap into the same Strength, Love, Mercy, Devine Light, and Joy of Christ the Lord as you have in your life?

Oh, my beloved sister how can I ever thank you for being a vessel that God can use in this way? For being in a smaller way a guiding light in this dark world?

For not only showing me but the world how to love God?
I pray to God that you find all the blessings God has for you this day and that he will give an extra portion of His love so you can continue to grow in the love of the God you have found!

Your loving brother.

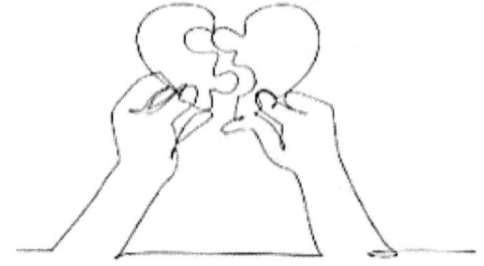

I Chose to Love You

I have seen the darkness that you hide from the world, and I still choose to love you.

I have seen the most hidden parts of your soul, and I still chose to love you.

I have seen you at the lowest points in your life and I not only chose to love you, but I decided to carry you in those times.

I have seen you crying in the night, and I not only chose to love you, but I chose to hold you tighter in my arms.

I have seen you hiding in the darkness trying to escape the light that I have provided for you. I have seen you on your knees praying, and I have seen you singing and dancing in my love.

No matter how far you are from me and no matter the state of your soul may be in I will always choose to love you, and I will always be by your side.

Take me

Oh Lord, from the darkness my heart calls out to You. Oh my Lord, hear my heart say unto You, "Take Me Lord because I am here to do Your Will. Oh Lord, it's written in the sacred scrolls of me to doing Your will, so take me and fulfill Your promises."

Oh Lord, you see me reaching out to You from the darkness. Oh Lord, you can hear my prayers to You calling out to You. So, take me into Your loving arms, hold me fast, and let me complete Your will this day.

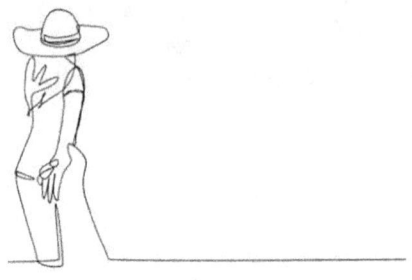

Take my Hand

I was sitting in the darkness of my sin, and I was waiting for the light to enter my life; when I heard You say to me, "Take My hand and I will carry you through your darkest night. I will carry you through the good, the bad, the ugly, and the pain of this life."

As I sat in that darkness and glum that I had made for myself and as I was listening to the words You had just spoken to me:

You once again said to me "Take my hand and I will show you the light of my love for you."

Oh, how my life changed that day as I took your hand looked into your face, and embraced the love You have for me. Oh, how that love filled my life and brought a new life and a new meaning to me.

Now that I have taken your hand, I no longer see the world through my eyes but see the world through Your love. And now that I have placed my life within those hands the world sees that same light within me.

So, I encourage you to reach out and take the hand that He is offering you so that you can find the light of His love for you.

Every night

Every night, I lie in bed and close my eyes and I can see the world that is waiting for me.

Every night, I go through the door where no one has been before, to a world that I can call my own.

Every night, I see a vision of that world only to be affirmed by just how deep Your love for me goes.

Every night, I dream of a world that is filled with God's love and grace.

Every night, I dream of a world where all sorrow, pain, and hatred have been wiped away.

Angels Sing

The day you were born I heard the angels sing, and my life changed thereafter, and as I held your tinny form and was looking upon that angelic face my heart felt like it would burst from all the love that I have just for you.

The day that you were born God smiled down on you and gave you all His love. Then the Angels lifted their voices once again and praised God for the miracle He had performed.

Your Love Lifts Me Up

You once told me that there would be a day when all the lonely days that I have gone through would come to an end.

I now know that you ended all that by wrapping your love around me and it's for this reason that I can't get you out of my head.

Your love for me has lifted me to new heights, and your love for me has saved me from a life of loneliness and misery,

There is one truth I have discovered and that is your love for me has changed things for the better.

For that alone I must now thank you. Thank you for helping me find the loving and caring person that I have become today. Thank you for giving me a portion of your strength so that I could weather the storms that came into my life. Thank you for being the companion that I needed. Thank you for just being you.

I will love you

You can never say that I just walked away from you because I will always love you. I will love you with every breath I will ever take. I will love you when you are far from me and I will love you when I grow old and forget my name.

When I gave you my heart I discovered a new song within my heart and that song will continue to play in my heart till the sun no longer shines.

You helped to transform the house we lived in; into more than walls of stone and You helped me make it a home of love.

Remembering you is easy, I do it every day. Missing you is the heartache that never goes away.
but the knowledge that someday we will be reunited makes all the difference in the world.

Little House

Every night I dream of living in a little house that looks over a valley.

I can see myself raising my family in that little house, and I can always see my spouse and I growing old in that same little house.

In my little house, I would teach my children the love of God, and I would show them all the wonders He has provided for them.

Oh Lord, thank you for giving me my little house just beyond the valley which is filled with God, love, and family even if it's only in my dreams.

Letting Go of the Father's hand

Sometimes we lose our way by letting go of the Father's hands.

Wasting our time in the dark doing our own thing, blind to the guiding light.

Never leaving our side waiting for us to return to the Father's loving hands.

The Father always asks me when I return to Him "Do you want my love, do you want me to walk with you, do you want forgiveness? If you do take my hand and come with me.

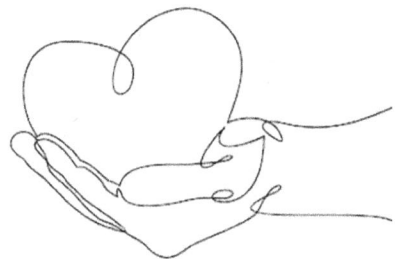

Evidence of my Love

You don't have to look very far to find evidence of the love I have for you, because my love for you is written in these very words.

Yes, my child I have written my love for you in the heavens above your head, and from star to star that is the vastness of my love for you

Oh, my child don't you know that I have even written my love for you from the sound of crashing waves of the ocean to the rising sun.

Yes, my child I have written my love for you in a single raindrop to the raging storm, and I have written my love for you in the tender embrace of your mother.

And finally, my child the most important evidence of my love for is written on the heart of every living creature in the world.

Fingerprints

Oh, how can I not rejoice when I see God's fingerprints all through my life? Oh, how can I not see the pattern of God's fingerprints weaving throughout my life?

Oh, how can I not rejoice when I see those same fingerprints in my family's life, in my daily life, and in the simplest little thing that may cross my path?

Oh, how can I not be amazed when I see how you have shaped my life from your living Word?

Oh, how can I not see that You have never forgotten, never forsaken, never abandoned. And not for a second have I not felt safe in Your hands

Oh, how can I not see that You are always and forever working in my heart, and how can I not see that there will never come a day when You're not holding me together?

Oh, can I not see all these things that You have shown me in the sunrise in the morning, in the stars above my head at night, in the laughter of a child, in the gentle simmer rain, and that I know Your risen Son.

Distant stars

Somewhere beyond all those distant stars, You, oh Lord have chosen me to love even in my unworthy state.

Somewhere beyond all those distant stars, You, oh Lord have set my heart afire. And You oh Lord have chosen to open my eyes so that I can see the truth.

Somewhere beyond all those distant stars, You, oh Lord have chosen to guide my every step. And you oh Lord have chosen to walk with me.

Somewhere beyond all those distant stars, You, oh Lord are waiting with open arms for me to come to You.

Somewhere beyond all those distant stars, You, oh Lord guard my soul, and You oh Lord remain in control of all creation.

Hallelujah and Amen!!!!

Quite of the Night

In the quiet of the night, I whisper my cares into your ear, and I whisper my love for you.

I whisper into your ear that you will always see the person you need me to be.

I whisper into your ear "Please don't leave me on that day when my strength finely fades on me."

Please Don't hesitate to take the love that I whispered into your ear because I have found that the long shadows of time are rapidly approaching me and my time is quickly coming to an end.

What I have whispered into your ear is a living thing, and there is over welling evidence of it because my love for you is written in the stars.

Divine Illumination

Beyond the horizon lies a better life, revealed through His eyes, free from strife. In the stillness of the night, His presence was clear, guiding through trials, and erasing fear.

His light shines bright in the darkest hour, leading with unwavering power. With each step taken, His grace abides, and in His presence, all fear subsides.

Through every trial, His hand I hold, His love, a beacon, steadfast and bold. With faith unwavering, I journey on, towards the horizon, where His promise dawns.

Embracing Eternity

In the vast expanse of eternity amidst twilight's embrace, I have journeyed beyond the stars seeking my place.

Fate's hand led me to you, where your love has nurtured me and I have grown as a person within your essence.

Across the horizon where time dissolves your presence has guided me through life's challenges and has offered a steady light on the darkest nights.

In your gaze, I have discovered my true worth and with you, I have bloomed and soared to be more than I ever thought I could be.

Together within our sanctuary your love eternally resides filling the void I once sought to fill near and far.

Your essence inspires me to delve deeper into myself, striving to become the person you deserve.

Steadfast Companion (1)

In the tumult of life's stormy sea,

When the world spins, uncertain, wild, and free,

Just reach out, grasp my hand, you'll see,

and I'll guide you through, unerringly.

In your darkest hour, when shadows loom, And

hope seems lost in the gloom,

Hold tight, and don't let despair consume you,

Together, we'll brave the tempest's boom.

Through life's journey, wherever you roam, Know

you're never truly alone,

For by your side, I'll steadfastly roam, With

open arms, I'll welcome you home.

Steadfast Companion (2)

In a moment of chaos, when your world flips upside down,
Know you can always find stability in me, Reach out, grasp my hand, and hold on tight.
In the tumult of life's stormy sea,
When the world spins, uncertain, wild, and free,
Just reach out, grasp my hand, you'll see,
and I'll guide you through, unerringly.
Through the twists and turns, I'll guide you right,
Never faltering, never leading astray,
Just trust in me, and hold on tight.
In your darkest hour, when shadows loom,
And hope seems lost in the gloom,
Hold tight, and don't let despair consume you,
Together, we'll brave the tempest's boom.
In the depths of your darkest day,
When the storm rages within,
I'll be your anchor, your steadfast friend,
Just hold on to me, through thick and thin.
Through life's journey, wherever you roam,
Know you're never truly alone,
For by your side, I'll steadfastly roam,
With open arms, I'll welcome you home.
Wherever your journey leads, whatever the strife,
Rest assured, I won't abandon your side,
With arms wide open, I'll welcome you in,
So hold on to me, and let our bond abide.

Eternal Yearning

Don't you know that in the vastness of eternity, I patiently await your return to me?

Don't you know that I understand the depths of your despair when you wander the darkness?

Oh, how my heart aches as I watch you wander as if a soul adrift in time and space.

Don't you feel the warmth of my love, yearning to pull you from the shadows?

Can you sense my outstretched hand, waiting for yours to intertwine with mine?

I know that your path may look uncertain and troubled, but my unwavering love remains.

So, come to me and take my hand and together, in love, we will overcome all trials and fears.

Ethereal Odyssey

In the vast expanse of eternity, I await amidst cosmic waves and the embrace of twilight, longing for your presence to fill the void.

Whether it be the arrival of my soul mate or the divine touch of God's hand, I hold onto hope.

Across the horizon where time dissolves, I search for the answers to life's mysteries, seeking purpose and understanding in the boundless expanse.

Guided by the gentle whispers of eternity's embrace, I navigate the endless space in pursuit of belonging.

In the realm of sight, I strive to find my place, drawing closer to the essence of existence with each passing moment.

Trusting in the eternal journey that awaits, I find solace and courage in the twilight's embrace, embracing the unknown with open arms.

Divine Nature's Embrace

Oh, how I love the feeling of the warm summer rain falling upon my face. I love how It feels when it runs down through my hair and onto my body.

Oh, how that feeling reminds me of how my Savior's love washes over me and cleanses me of all my sins.

Oh, how I love the feeling of the warmth of the morning sun upon my face, I love the way its warmth spreads throughout my body.

Oh, how that feeling reminds me of how my God's warmth lives in me.

Oh, how I love the sound of the birds singing in the trees, I love the way it makes my day so much better.

Oh, how I love the way these songs remind me to praise and sing of God's glory to all the world.

Oh, how I cherish these moments, where nature's embrace mirrors the divine love that surrounds me.

Sacred Tapestry

In the tapestry of life, you're the divine artistry,
That is who you are to me, my true soul's affinity.
Like a whisper from above, you came into view,
A gift from God, so pure and true.
Before you, my love, I wandered lost and blind,
But in your presence, solace I find.
You're the answer to prayers I never knew I'd spoken,
A testament to the love that's unbroken.
In your eyes, I see a reflection divine,
A bond forged by a hand greater than mine.
Together, we walk in grace and light,
Guided by love, through the darkest night.
With you, my soul finds its destined mate,
A journey blessed by fate.
In your embrace, I am whole and complete,
With God's grace, our love will never retreat.

Echoes of the Soul

In the silence, solitude abides, Heartbreak's
weight, where hope subsides. Trapped
within the confines of despair, No solace
found, no answer fair.
Alone, I wander through this night,
Where shadows dance in muted light.
God's presence, distant and unclear,
Lost in the echoes of my fear.
A prisoner of my own design, Bound
by chains of doubt and time. Yet in
the stillness, a whisper stirs, A faint
reminder, hope endures.
Though darkness cloaks the path I roam,
Within my heart, a flicker, home.
For even in this endless night,
A glimmer of faith, a distant light.
Though trials may come, and darkness loom,
Know that even in the deepest gloom,
God's love remains, a steadfast rope,
An anchor for the soul in times of no hope.

Whispers of Love

In the quiet whispers of the night, I tried to tell you,
Of the depths within, where my love grew,
For you are the one who completes me whole,
The essence of my being, the depth of my soul.
Before your presence graced my days,
I wandered lost in life's endless maze,
But with you by my side, I stand tall and true,
For you are the light that guides me through.
In the echoes of our shared embrace,
I find solace, a sacred space,
Where loneliness fades, replaced by bliss,
As I cherish the love we both reminisce.
You are the melody to my silent song,
The strength within when the world feels wrong,
With you, I've conquered every strife,
For in your love, I've found my life.
So here I stand, with you, hand in hand,
Bound by a love that forever expands,
You've lifted me from the depths of despair,
And together, we soar beyond compare.

A Journey from Loneliness to Hope

You, my love, embody the essence of divine grace in my life. Before you, the torrent of loneliness rained in my soul like a raging storm, casting me into the valley of death.

But now, with you by my side, I stand whole, lifted from the depths and planted firmly on the mountain of hope.

Your presence is a beacon of God's love, guiding me through the darkest of nights and illuminating the path to salvation.

In your embrace, I find solace, as you are the steadfast anchor in the tumultuous sea of life.

Together, we stand as true soulmates, united in the eternal warmth of God's love, transcending all challenges and trials.

Eternal Devotion

From the first touch of your hand, my heart declared its allegiance to you,

And from the day I said "I do" my heart sang "I am yours forevermore yes I am yours for all eternity."

Oh, forevermore, in every pulse, in every breath, I am fiercely and wholly yours.

And so, as long as the stars continue to dance in the night sky, my love for you will burn brighter with each passing moment.

For in every beat of my heart, in every whisper of my soul, I am forever and completely yours.

Song for over the horizon

(Verse 1)
Somewhere over the horizon, My true love is waiting,
In the golden hues of dawn, Her silhouette captivating.

(Chorus)
Just this side of eternity, She waits for me,
With her arms spread wide, Waiting to give.

(Verse 2)
In the whispers of the wind, I hear her tender sighs,
In every star that shines, I see the love in her eyes.

(Chorus)
Just this side of eternity, She waits for me,
With her arms spread wide,

Waiting to give.

(Bridge)
Time may stretch its arms,
But our love knows no bounds, Through every trial and storm, Her love forever surrounds.

(Chorus)
Just this side of eternity, She waits for me,
With her arms spread wide, Waiting to give.

(Outro)
And when at last we meet,
In the realm where dreams collide, We'll dance through eternity,
With love as our guide.

Verse 1:
| E | F# | G#m | F# | E | B | C#m | F# | B |

Somewhere over the horizon, my true love is waiting.
| E | F# | G#m | F# | E | B | C#m | F# | B |

In the golden hues of dawn, her silhouette captivating.

Chorus:
| E | F# | G#m | F# | E | B | C#m | F# | B |

Just this side of eternity, she waits for me.
| E | F# | G#m | F# | E | B | C#m | F# | B |

With her arms spread wide, waiting to give.

Verse 2:
| E | F# | G#m | F# | E | B | C#m | F# | B |

In the whispers of the wind, I hear her tender sighs.
| E | F# | G#m | F# | E | B | C#m | F# | B |

In every star that shines, I see the love in her eyes.

Chorus:
| E | F# | G#m | F# | E | B | C#m | F# | B |

Just this side of eternity, she waits for me.
| E | F# | G#m | F# | E | B | C#m | F# | B |

With her arms spread wide, waiting to give.

Bridge:
| A | B | E | C#m |

Time may stretch its arms,
| A | B | E | C#m |

But our love knows no bounds.
| A | B | E | C#m |

Through every trial and storm,
| A | B | E | C#m |

Her love forever surrounds.

Chorus:
E   F#   G#m F#   E   B   C#m F#   B
Just this side of eternity, she waits for me.
E   F#   G#m F#   E   B   C#m F#   B
With her arms spread wide, waiting to give.

Outro:
E   F#   G#m F#   E   B   C#m F#   B
And when at last we meet,

E   F#   G#m F#   E   B   C#m F#   B
In the realm where dreams collide.
E   F#   G#m F#   E   B   C#m F#   B
We'll dance through eternity,

For piano played at 4/4

1st
E   F#   G#m F#   E   B   C#m F#   B
| E
| | F# | G#m | F# | E | B | C#m | F# | B

Chorus
E   F#   G#m F#   E   B   C#m F#   B
| E
| | F# | G#m | F# | E | B | C#m | F# | B

2nd
E   F#   G#m F#   E   B   C#m F#   B
| E
| | F# | G#m | F# | E | B | C#m | F# | B

Chorus
E   F#   G#m F#   E   B   C#m F#   B
| E | F# | G#m | F# | E | B | C#m | F# | B
|

Bridge
A   B   E   C#m
| A | B | E | C#m |
A   B   E   C#m
| A | B | E | C#m |
A   B   E   C#m
| A | B | E | C#m |
A   B   E   C#m
| A | B | E | C#m |

Chorus
E
| E
| F#
| F#   G#m
| G#m F#   E
| F#   B
| E   C#m   F#
| B | C#m B
| F#
| B

Outro
E   F#   G#m   F#   E   B   C#m   F#   B
| E
| E | F#
F# | G#m
G#m | F#
F#   E | E
B | B | C#m
C#m   F# | F#
B | B
| E
| E | F#
F# | G#m
G#m | F#
F#   E | E
B | B | C#m

```
C#m    F#     | F#
B      | B
| E
|      | F#    | G#m  | F#    | E     | B     | C#m  | F#    | B
```

God's Gift

From the very first time I met you; I believed that the tales I heard about you seemed to be things of people's imagination and that those who faithfully followed you were out of their minds.

To me, it seemed that the stories that I heard of how people who followed Your footsteps were guided by some unknown force and that it was like you could see every unseen danger that lay before them.

To me, it seemed that the stories of your strength, resolve, and, wisdom were beyond the understanding of my simple mind.

To me, it seemed that I was undeserving of anything you had to offer me, and I could not do anything to change how you saw me in your eyes.

Then you told me that all I had to do was, "Seek and I would find, ask and it would be given me, and knock and the door shall be opened unto you." "To all who are thirsty, I will give freely from the springs of the water of life."

Once I opened that door my eyes were opened, my mind was freed, and my life was transformed into a life of LIFE and not death.

Author's Message

I have laid my soul bare for you in these poems. I can only hope you will take each and every one of them into your heart and make a Season of Change within your life before it's too late.

I can only pray that you will seek out the gift God offers to you.

As I said before a season of change is coming to this world and I only can pray that you will make the right choice.

I can only pray that you will read and understand the following information. If you want a change in your life for the better, please follow these instructions.

The Plan of Salvation

Is anyone perfect?
As it is written, there is none righteous, no, not one. (Romans 3:10)

This means no one is perfect. Is

there any exception?
For all have sinned and come short of the glory of God. (Romans3:23)

None of us meet God's holy standards. Where

did sin come from?
Wherefore, as by one man sin entered into the world, and death by sin, and so death passed upon all men, for that all have sinned. (Romans 5:12)

Adam, the first person created by God, sinned and passed sin on to every human being.

What do we deserve for our sins?
For the wages of sin is death, but the gift of God is eternal life through Jesus Christ our Lord. (Romans 6: 23)

Because of our sins, we are supposed to die.

The Greater Travelers Rest Baptist Church E. Dewey Smith, Jr. Pastor/Teacher
4650 Flat Shoals Parkway Decatur, GA 30034
Telephone: 404-243-9336 • Fax: 404-212-1265

Who paid the price?

God commandeth his love toward us, in that, while we were yet sinners, Christ died for us.
(Romans 5: 8)
Instead of us dying, Jesus died in our place in order to give us life.

What is the way out?

That if thou shalt confess with thy mouth, the Lord Jesus, and shalt believe in thine heart God hath raised him from the dead thou shalt be saved. For with the heart, man believeth unto righteousness; and with the mouth, confession is made unto salvation. For the scripture saith, whosoever believeth on him shall not be ashamed. (Romans 10:9-10)

For whosoever shall call upon the name of the Lord shall be saved. (Romans 10:13)
Jesus is the only way out.

How can I get out?

By Salvation, which is as simple as A...B...C: A -

Admit you are a sinner

B - Believe in your heart that Jesus died and rose from the dead

C - Confess with your mouth that God raised Jesus from the dead, and that you accept Jesus Christ as the Lord of your life. And simply pray this prayer:

"Father, I know that I have broken your laws and my sins have separated me from you. I am truly sorry, and now I want to turn away from my past sinful life and turn toward you. Please forgive me, and help me avoid sinning again. I believe that your son, Jesus Christ, died for my sins, was resurrected from the dead, is alive, and hears my prayer. I invite Jesus to become the Lord of my life, to rule and reign in my heart from this day forward. Please send your Holy Spirit to help me obey You, and do your will for the rest of my life. In Jesus' name, I pray, Amen."

www.ingramcontent.com/pod-product-compliance
Lightning Source LLC
LaVergne TN
LVHW010221070526
838199LV00062B/4682